THE
GHOSTLY TALES
OF
CONNECTICUT

Published by Arcadia Children's Books
A Division of Arcadia Publishing
Charleston, SC
www.arcadiapublishing.com

Spooky America is a trademark of Arcadia Publishing, Inc.

First published 2020

Manufactured in the United States

ISBN 978-1-4671-9809-7
Library of Congress Control Number: 2020938908

Notice: The information in this book is true and complete to the best of our knowledge. It is offered without guarantee on the part of the author or Arcadia Publishing. The author and Arcadia Publishing disclaim all liability in connection with the use of this book.

Photo credits: used throughout Eugenia Petrovskaya/Shutterstock.com, Nataliia K/ Shutterstock.com, In-Finity/Shutterstock.com, vectorkuro/Shutterstock.com; p. iv–v the Hornbills Studio/Shutterstock.com, Caso Alfonso/Shutterstock.com, Ivakoleva/ Shutterstock.com, LDDesign/Shutterstock.com; p. vi, 68 Stone36/Shutterstock.com; p. 4, 80 andreiuc88/Shutterstock.com; p. 3 Elena Paletskaya/Shutterstock.com; p. 8–9 Pavel Kovaricek/Shutterstock.com; p. 12 Robert F. Balazik/Shutterstock.com; p. 15, 60, 71 Cattallina/Shutterstock.com; p. 16–17 Nosyrevy/Shutterstock.com; p. 18, 90 Ioana Catalina E/Shutterstock.com; p. 20–21 Stone36/Shutterstock.com; p. 25 KsanaGraphica/Shutterstock.com; p. 30 somnuk jansinka/Shutterstock.com; p. 36, 100 mythja/Shutterstock.com; p. 40–41 Vertyr/Shutterstock.com; p. 42 CHAIWATPHOTOS/ Shutterstock.com; p. 46 Mimadeo/Shutterstock.com; p. 50–51 Bodor Tivadar/ Shutterstock.com; p. 52, 102 VladimirCeresnak/Shutterstock.com; p. 54 Fer Gregory/ Shutterstock.com; p. 56–57 Sensay/Shutterstock.com; p. 66 Forgem/ Shutterstock.com; p. 76–77 Jurgita Batuleviciene/Shutterstock.com; p. 83 PHEANGPHOR studio/Shutterstock.com; p. 86–87 Barnabas Davoti/Shutterstock.com; p. 92–93 shaineast/Shutterstock.com; p. 95 Juncat/Shutterstock.com; p. 98 basel101658/ Shutterstock.com; p. 104–105 Ihnatovich Maryia/Shutterstock.com.

Spooky America

THE
GHOSTLY TALES
OF
CONNECTICUT

ELLIE O'RYAN

adapted from *Connecticut Ghost Stories and Legends* by Thomas D'Agostino and Arlene Nicholson

MASSACHUSETTS

NY

CONNECTICUT

NY

ATLANTIC OCEAN

TABLE OF CONTENTS & MAP KEY

Introduction

Connecticut is a state filled with natural wonders, from forests and mountains to rivers and waterfalls. It's a state steeped in history, from its Native American heritage to its status as one of the original thirteen colonies and the site of many important Revolutionary War battles.

It's also a state renowned for supernatural happenings and otherworldly haunts.

Connecticut has more legends and folklore than any other state in New England. Perhaps there is something about the landscape that causes supernatural occurrences to happen so often there.

Or perhaps it's something about the state's rich history. Spirits find themselves trapped to their past lives, unable to move on to the next world. They linger on, perhaps with unfinished business that haunts them. Perhaps with a story that they long to tell to someone, anyone, who might listen.

Lost lovers who long to be reunited. Witches who torment the countryside. Soldiers whose blood soaked into Connecticut soil. A mysterious hound with a message of doom. A headless horseman who gallops down the road with a burning fury and an uncompleted mission. A hideout that holds a secret history. A cemetery. A swamp. A buried treasure, a haunted island, and a pirate's curse.

They're all waiting for you in the Nutmeg State.

They're waiting for you in the pages of this book, too.

The Green Lady

It's a long road to the Seventh Day Baptist Cemetery. A road with twists and turns; a road with some bumps and some bends.

It's also a road with its very own ghost.

She's called the Green Lady.

The Green Lady walks the road each night, back and forth, back and forth, surrounded by a green mist that glows, softly, in the darkness. Some who have seen the Green Lady say that her dress, an elegant shade of emerald green, looks as beautiful as it did the day she died wearing it.

Others say that her dress isn't green at all. They've seen the Green Lady covered in muck and mire from the swamp where she died. The slimy tendrils trail behind her but never leave a mark in the road.

In life, her name was Elisabeth Palmiter. We know that she was thirty years old when she died. We know when she died—on April 12, 1800.

What we don't know, exactly, is *how* she died.

There are a few stories about her untimely end.

This is one of them.

Winter had lasted longer than anyone had expected—but at last, the warm sun was shining. Finally, the tiny green leaves had begun to unfurl on the trees. Snowdrops and crocuses peeked out of the dirt, whispering a promise of all the flowers yet to bloom.

Elizabeth Palmiter couldn't wait.

There were other things that couldn't wait, either. Chores at the sprawling house she shared with her husband, Matthew, needed attention. And there was a long list of supplies that they needed from town. They decided to divide and conquer: Matthew would journey to town while Elizabeth stayed home to begin spring cleaning.

Their separation that day would prove to be fatal.

Elizabeth waved from the porch as Matthew began the walk down the winding road, past the swamp and the cemetery. Then she pushed up the sleeves of her pretty green dress—it was Matthew's favorite; he always said it brought out the green in her eyes—and got right to work.

First Elizabeth opened the windows to give the house a good airing—there was nothing like that sweet springtime air—and kept herself busy with baking. Two loaves of bread; a pie; a cake. The pie she cooled on the windowsill. It smelled delicious, but she wouldn't have a bite, not even a nibble of the crust, until Matthew returned and they could enjoy it together.

Then Elizabeth turned her attention to the chores. Dusting and sweeping; mending and folding; she was so busy that she didn't notice, at first, that the light had begun to dim unusually early. When she shivered, she reached for a shawl. But soon the wind was gusting with such force that even Elizabeth couldn't ignore it any longer. When she glanced outside, Elizabeth was shocked to see the heavy gray sky and the thick clouds that had blocked the sun. Even the branches of the trees seemed to be shivering. Or perhaps they were trembling, afraid of what was to come.

Elizabeth ran through the house, closing one window after another against the chill. She'd need to bring in more wood for the fire— to put the heavy quilts back on the bed—

But first, the pie!

She reached the kitchen window and pulled in the pie just as the first snowflakes started falling. In minutes, the ground was covered with a thin white layer. If only that had been all, she wouldn't have worried quiet so much.

But the snow grew heavier, and Matthew still wasn't home.

Elizabeth wrapped another shawl around her shoulders and stepped outside. She should've seen blossoms dancing on a gentle breeze, not hard, glittering snowflakes swirling on a wind that seemed almost angry.

There was no denying it: an April blizzard had struck, with her here at home, and Matthew—where was he? In town, safe at the store?

Or already on the road?

"Matthew," she might have whispered as worry gnawed at her heart.

She paced the porch, watching the road until the snow had piled so high that she could no longer distinguish it from the rest of the landscape. Was Matthew trudging home to her on that snow-packed road? As the sky darkened and night loomed, with not even moon nor stars for light?

She couldn't bear the thought.

Elizabeth reached inside the house for two things: her warm woolen cloak and the lantern they kept by the door. She'd set off for town and meet Matthew on the road. Together, with the light of the lantern, they'd find their way home, where the fire would be crackling and supper waiting for them to share it. The pie, of course, was for dessert.

Like shards of ice, the snowflakes stung as they pelted her cheeks, but Elizabeth forged ahead. Her feet felt the cold keenly, even through her boots; soon her toes went numb and she stumbled with almost every step.

Not even the trusty lantern could shine

brightly enough to cut through the swirling snow. Elizabeth paused. A momentary flash of doubt plagued her. Was she still on the road? Was she still headed toward town? There were turns in the road, especially near the swamp, but Elizabeth had walked this road so many times. Surely she would know—surely she would sense it—if she went astray.

She might've, too, if her feet hadn't been so numb from the cold. She would've noticed the swamp water as it seeped through the soles of

her boots. But Elizabeth didn't feel the water until it reached her calves. The iciness of it made her gasp.

Her heart was pounding, but Elizabeth took a deep breath and tried to calm herself. It was just a misstep. Just a wrong turn. She'd turn around and right herself—get back on the path—find Matthew—

But with her next step, Elizabeth's foot plunged into the thick, cloying mud. She tried to pull up her leg, but the swamp mud wouldn't give it up. With a sickening, sucking noise, her leg suddenly pulled free—leaving her boot behind. The freezing mud had hardened like cement. Her boot was lost to it.

Limping, Elizabeth tried to take another step, but the swamp waters only deepened. She turned one way, then the other, searching for a landmark, a sign, a familiar sight that might tell her where she was.

That might tell her which way to go.

The swamp waters crept up her woolen cloak, making it so heavy that she felt like it was dragging her down. She shrugged it off, but the waters were seeping into her dress, too, her pretty green dress. It wasn't so bright now. It wasn't so pretty anymore.

"Matthew!" she might have cried, but the howling winds snatched away her voice so that no one ever heard the last word she spoke.

For his part, Matthew was warm and dry in town. He'd spotted the storm's sudden approach and had the good sense to stay the night at the inn. The fire was roaring, and a thick, hearty stew bubbled in the stewpot. Such unexpected April snow squalls wouldn't last long, Matthew knew. He felt certain he'd be on his way home to Elizabeth at first light.

Of course, the journey home took him longer than usual. The sun was shining brightly once more, transforming the thick drifts of snow into slushy puddles. He whistled a little, eager to see his bride after their night apart.

It was the dress he saw first. Unmistakable, that green dress, the only one like it in the county. Why, he wondered, was Elizabeth's favorite dress floating in the middle of the swamp? Then he saw the strands of auburn hair. The feet, one in a stocking, one in a boot.

That's when, with a crushing sense of grief, Matthew knew that he would never see Elizabeth again.

He was only half right, though. The Elizabeth he'd known in life, his love, was gone forever.

But that very night, the Green Lady rose from the swamp to continue searching for the man she loved. Rambling up and down the road to town, a pleasant smile flickering on her face. Surely they'd meet soon. Just a bit farther, perhaps. Just around the bend.

And so she has traveled that road for more than 200 years, still searching for her husband,

even though he departed this earthly realm long, long ago. Some who've seen the Green Lady in their travels have sworn they've seen the ghost of Matthew, too, searching for his wife. But if both spirits have been traversing the same stretch of road, past the cemetery, past the swamp, past their old home, how come they still haven't found each other?

Will they ever?

CHAPTER 2

The Black Dog of the Hanging Hills

The Hanging Hills are a mountain range that includes the town of Meridian. For hundreds of years, people have visited the Hanging Hills to appreciate their rare natural beauty, from the rivers and reservoirs that contain clear, cool water to the unique rock formations made from volcanic rock. People aren't the only ones drawn to the Hanging Hills, though. There are many common creatures that inhabit the Hanging

Hills mountain range: squirrels, chipmunks, deer, rabbits, owls, and hawks.

There is also an extraordinarily uncommon creature who dwells within the Hanging Hills.

The Black Dog.

This is, of course, no ordinary dog, but a strange and otherworldly beast that has been spotted in the Hanging Hills for more than a century. It is not especially large, nor especially fearsome. When the Black Dog opens its mouth, no sound comes out. Not a bark, not a howl, not a growl.

Just a strange, spooky mist that rises into the air and hangs there, quivering, until it fades into nothingness.

The Black Dog has roamed the Hanging Hills for so long that many hikers, explorers, and naturalists have seen it and lived to tell the tale.

At least, some of them did.

In 1898, a young geologist named W.H.C. Pynchon set off on an expedition to study the unique rock formations of the Hanging Hills. His studies at Harvard had prepared him well for field work in the mountain range.

Or so he thought.

While Pynchon hiked the trails of the West Peak, he suddenly had the strangest sense that he was being…followed. He hadn't seen anyone else in the hills. No hikers or naturalists or picnickers. There was just peace…and quiet…

And that unshakeable sense that someone—or something—was behind him.

Pynchon rubbed his neck. He wouldn't turn around to look. That would be foolish, and he was a man of science. He believed in facts and truth, ideas that were as sturdy as the rocks he had dedicated his life to studying.

And yet, with every step, the feeling grew.

It was nonsense, Pynchon knew, but he couldn't stop himself. At last, he turned around…

And spotted a hound in the middle of the trail.

Pynchon let out a short bark of a laugh. He

was more relieved than he wanted to admit. After all, imagining that something was following him wasn't his style.

Besides, he liked dogs.

Pynchon bent forward with his hands on his knees and whistled. Maybe he called out, "Here, pup. Here, doggie."

Unlike all the other dogs Pynchon had befriended over the years, the black dog didn't move.

Perhaps it was shy. Perhaps it had spent its whole life alone in the Hanging Hills and was unfamiliar with the friendship that could grow between a man and his dog. Pynchon decided to walk a little farther and see if the dog would follow.

It did.

Pynchon didn't mind. He was pleased to have a little company on the journey, even if the shy dog seemed to keep its distance. It was a fine-looking creature, just the right size for a dog, and well-behaved, too. Not once did Pynchon notice it bark at a squirrel or stray from the path to chase a rabbit through the brush.

By late afternoon, Pynchon's knapsack had grown heavy with samples and his feet had begun to ache. Darkness was falling; it would be best to leave the mountainside before it got too late. Even as he began his descent, the dog kept pace with him.

As Pynchon reached the edge of the wooded area, he wondered if his new friend would continue to accompany him. He almost hoped it would. Over just the course of a few hours, he'd grown fond of the dog. He wouldn't mind its company on a regular basis.

He turned around to whistle for the pup to come, only to see that a large gap had grown between them. The black dog was just beyond the tree line. Waiting. Watching.

Pynchon decided to try one more time. He whistled and softly snapped his fingers. "Here, pup. Come here!"

The black dog cocked its head and stared straight at Pynchon. Then, it lifted its head to the sky and howled. But no sound came out of its mouth—just a faint whiff of vapor that spread through the air like a contagion.

Pynchon frowned. It was chilly, but not so cold that the dog's breath should form such a cloud. He'd never know a dog to be voiceless before, but he supposed it was possible. He walked forward, glancing occasionally over his shoulder only to see the black dog disappear among the trees.

It would be three years before Pynchon returned to the Hanging Hills. This time, he brought a friend. Herbert Marshall was a geologist, too. He worked for the US Geological Survey. Marshall was no stranger to the wonders of the Hanging Hills. He'd journeyed there many times before, and Pynchon was looking forward to traveling with an expert.

He was also looking forward to seeing if the black dog still roamed the mountainside.

The night before they began their ascent into the Hanging Hills, the two travelers shared a meal at the inn where they were staying. Pynchon ventured to tell Marshall about the black dog he had seen on his last journey.

"I know that dog!" Marshall may have replied, with a note of excitement in his voice. "He's famous, you know."

"Is he?" Pynchon asked. He sipped his piping-hot coffee.

"The Black Dog of the Hanging Hills," Marshall said. "Legend has it that the first time you view him, good fortune awaits. After the second viewing, the shadow of misfortune hangs over you. And after the third sight of the Black Dog . . ."

Marshall's voice trailed off.

"What happens?" Pynchon prompted him.

"You die," Marshall replied.

A look of alarm must have crossed Pynchon's face, for Marshall chuckled and clapped his friend on the back. "It's only a legend. A tale to frighten children around the campfire. I've seen the Black Dog twice before and I've no worries. Not a one."

Pynchon laughed, too. "I can't say I recall any examples of good fortune after I saw the beast," he replied. "I'm sure you're right. A tall tale, and nothing more."

The next morning dawned bitterly cold, but the skies were clear. That was a blessing, Pynchon thought. Wintertime mountain treks were possible with the appropriate supplies, but poor weather made them too treacherous to undertake the risk.

The friends didn't say much as they scaled the south side of the West Peak. Snow had accumulated in the cracks and crevices of the mountainside. Once again, Pynchon was grateful to follow in the footsteps of such an experienced mountaineer.

The higher they climbed, the deeper the crevices. Some were so shadowy that Pynchon had a feeling they would hold tight to the snow within them all year long, even through the fiercest summer heat. Pynchon stared deep into the crevices and felt, for the briefest moment, that he was staring into the valley of the shadow of death he had read about so often in the Bible. He was about to mention it to Marshall when his friend suddenly stopped.

"I see it," Marshall may have said. "The Black Dog."

Pynchon looked up and saw it, too. The Black Dog stood at the top of the summit, staring down upon them. Its eyes gleamed, just slightly, in the cold gray light.

The Black Dog opened his mouth, perhaps to yawn, perhaps to sigh, and the vapor trailed out, twisting into the sky. The beast made no noise.

There was a sound, though. A garbled sort of choking noise, as if one's throat had spasmed from fear. Pynchon turned to Marshall in

concern, only to see that his friend's face had gone deathly pale.

"Ididnotbelieveitbefore,butIbelieveitnow," Marshall said in a strangled-sounding voice.

Even as the words escaped from Marshall's mouth, Pynchon heard something new: the sound of rock rolling on rock.

What happened next was over in an instant yet seemed to take interminably long. It was a series of moments that Pynchon would relive again and again in the years to come.

Marshall's eyes widened. His arms flailed. His mouth formed the shape of a perfect O— but like the Black Dog, no sound came out.

Then, as the rocks under his feet continued to roll away, Marshall plunged down the mountainside.

It was over so fast.

"Marshall!" Pynchon must have screamed, his voice high and hollow. The only sound was the bone-chilling rattle of rocks tumbling down the mountainside.

Pynchon cried out for his friend again. But once more, there was no response.

The Black Dog stood above, watching in silence.

Pynchon knew one thing and one thing only in those first terrible moments following Marshall's fall: He needed to get help, and he needed to get it *now*.

Climbing as carefully and as cautiously as he could, Pynchon somehow managed to safely descend the West Peak. He ran, stumbling, to the nearest guidepost. Breathing heavily, the words escaped in staccato—"My friend—fall—West Peak—"

A sympathetic soul put a blanket around Pynchon's shoulders. Someone pressed a cup of tea into his hands, but he was shaking so much it spilled on the floor. He sat quietly as a search party was organized. As they were about to depart, Pynchon rose to his feet.

"I want to come," he might have said.

"Best to let the rescue squad search for your friend," the ranger told him, firmly but kindly. "We have experience with rescues in the Hanging Hills. You've had a shock—stay, and rest . . ."

Pynchon didn't argue. He wanted to help search for Marshall and bring him back to the inn, but he already knew he wouldn't be much use.

As it turned out, the search for Marshall wasn't much use, either. They followed Pynchon's directions to the letter and found Marshall's body, bent and broken, at the bottom of the ravine. As best they could tell, he had died instantly.

The Black Dog watched as the rescuers carried the dead man home.

It would be six long years before Pynchon returned to the Hanging Hills. Six years of distance. Six years of forgetting. After all, he was a man of science. Pynchon didn't let children's tales stand between him and his work. He didn't want to let his project in the Hanging Hills go unfinished for the rest of his career.

Not much had changed since his last visit to the Hanging Hills, but Pynchon pushed the memories from his mind. Still, at some elemental level, he knew that his choice was not without risk. The night before his final journey up the mountainside, he sat alone in his room and wrote the following words:

"I must die sometime. When I am gone, this paper may be of interest to those who remain, for, in throwing light on the manner of my death, it will also throw light on the end of the many victims that the old volcanic hills have claimed."

What happened to Pynchon next is a mystery that no man living will ever uncover. We know that he never returned to the inn where he was staying. We know that it would be many weeks before his body was found, frozen solid in the same place where Marshall had died six years before. There were no witnesses to Pynchon's fall, or his death.

Except, perhaps, the Black Dog.

CHAPTER 3

The Headless Horseman of Canton

The town of Canton is quaint and charming.

It never deserved to be the site of a such a gruesome crime.

Some tourists visit Canton to kayak on the Farmington River. Others come to browse in the antique shops. And some are drawn to hike the nature trails or the abandoned railway.

All of them must beware the Headless Horseman of Canton.

He rides on the darkest nights, driving his ghostly steed at a furious pace. The horse's eyes glow bright red, flickering as though they were made of flames. Its hooves pound the road but make no noise—making it all the easier for the Headless Horseman to sneak up on those who are unsuspecting. A cloak of mist, which seems to appear and disappear at will, also helps the Headless Horseman take his victims by surprise. Many drivers have had to swerve unexpectedly to avoid a collision when the Headless Horseman suddenly appears before them in all his haunting glory.

But who was this unfortunate soul who departed from this earth in such a violet and grisly manner?

His name has been lost to history, but his terrible ending reverberates through Canton still, like a haunting echo that no one can escape. In the year of 1781, as the Revolutionary War neared its end, a young French lieutenant had an important task. As an ally of the Revolutionaries, the brave lieutenant usually had no reason to fear travel through Connecticut.

But this night was different.

The lieutenant was also a paymaster. It was his responsibility to pay the soldiers, so he carried heavy leather saddlebags filled with money for the men at Saratoga. As night fell and his horse grew tired, the lieutenant had no choice but to stop at Dudley Case's tavern. A hot meal, a night's sleep, and he'd be on the road at first light, riding fast to make his important deliveries.

At least, that's what should have happened.

His boots echoed as he walked across the tavern's wooden floor. All the regular patrons turned to look at the stranger in his fine uniform.

The faint clink coming from his saddlebags was unmistakable.

"Evening, friend," Dudley Case might have said. "What brings you to these parts?"

The French lieutenant smiled apologetically and said a few words with a heavy accent. It was clear to all that he didn't speak much English.

He was a stranger to them. A stranger in every way.

Case was solicitous. He served the French lieutenant a hot meal, then escorted him to a private room for the night. Before he shut the door, the lieutenant, in his fragmented English, requested that Case wake him at dawn.

Case was only too happy to oblige.

The lieutenant, however, was never seen again.

At least, not alive.

According to Case, the lieutenant had left the tavern at first light, not even lingering for a cup of coffee or a bite to eat. The regular customers accepted Case's report at face value. They could only imagine what it might be like to carry such vast sums of money, even if only for a night. The sound of clinking coins from the bags would long live in their memory.

Several weeks later, though, a search party of French and American soldiers arrived at

Case's Tavern. The officers had many questions about the missing lieutenant—for he had never reached Saratoga.

Indeed, since his arrival at Case's Tavern, he had never been seen again.

The officers painstakingly interviewed everyone at and around Case's Tavern, but despite their diligence, no trace of the French lieutenant was found.

As for his part, Dudley Case spent the rest of his days living in prosperity. Folks in town often wondered how the Case family had acquired such riches, especially when everyone else had fallen on hard times.

Townspeople wondered about that, just as they wondered about the ghostly apparition, cloaked in mist, that had begun to appear along the road on moonless nights. The gaping hole where the ghost's head should be is what truly horrifies any soul so unlucky to cross paths with the Headless Horseman.

It wasn't until 1874—almost one hundred years later—that a grisly discovery revealed one possible clue about what had happened to the French lieutenant. The tavern had a devastating fire and was destroyed. Half-buried in the tavern's lonely basement was a skeleton, discovered only when a crew of volunteers arrived to clean up the smoldering remains of the building. Strangely, a human skull was found in another section of the cellar, leading the crew to believe that someone had met a most unfortunate end here in Case's Tavern.

Could those bones belong to the long-lost lieutenant?

The human remains found in the tavern were given a proper burial. But was that enough to set his soul at rest? If they truly did belong to the French lieutenant, is he finally at peace? It seems not.

The Headless Horseman will not rest until he completes his urgent mission.

The Headless Horseman will not rest.

CHAPTER 4

The Witches of Nineveh Falls

Nineveh Falls, in Killingworth, Connecticut, are as breathtakingly beautiful as they are deadly. It is no wonder that such a hauntingly lovely place has been the sight of so many horrors. The rocky sides of the ravine, the slippery rocks, the fast-flowing waters, and the jagged stones can spell danger for the living.

Indeed, for too many people, they have spelled doom.

For some, the dark history of Nineveh Falls

has been part of the appeal. There is a long legacy of witchcraft in the area. In the gloomy woods near the Connecticut River, witches were said to meet in secret, brewing vile concoctions in their cauldrons and chanting evil spells in the shadows.

Two of them, according to legend, were Goody Wee and Betty Wee.

When Goody Wee held her infant daughter, Betty, in her arms, did she already plan to teach her baby to chant spells and place curses along with learning her alphabet and her numbers?

When other mothers taught their daughters to cook, did Goody Wee teach Betty to brew potions?

When other little girls gathered wildflowers, did Betty harvest poisonous herbs and deadly toadstools?

We will never know exactly how Goody Wee tempted her daughter to join her in the dark arts. But the evil pair is still spoken about in voices of hushed horror, for their nightly cavorts to torment goodly people are remembered still.

According to legend, the Wee witches skulked through the lands, entering any home at will— even if all the doors and windows were locked.

For sport, they would spoil the finest cream so that butter could not be churned from it.

Of course, the Wee witches were not the cause of all the troubles that lurked around Nineveh Falls. Unseen spirits plagued the paths and roads, leading to tragic ends. Near the end of the nineteenth century, a local woman was out for a picturesque drive in her horse-drawn carriage when the unthinkable happened. Some supernatural force, unseen but potent, frightened her horse so terribly that he began to buck and pull at the reins. No mortal could control an animal so possessed by terror, and onlookers could do nothing but watch in horror as the horse galloped out of control, straight toward the bridge. The woman's panicked screams ricocheted off the rocks as the horse's eyeballs widened and rolled about in their sockets. She pulled on the reins so hard that the leather straps cut into her palms, but it was no use. There was no stopping the horse, who ran straight at the wooden railing—no pause,

no hesitation. The rail splintered into shards of wood that rained down into the waters below as the horse, the carriage, and the woman careened over the edge.

None survived.

If that tragic accident wasn't caused by the Wee witches, it was only because they kept busy with their own mischief along the roadway. Every merchant and farmer knew that the Wee witches traversed the roads in gleeful

search of their next victim. Every merchant and farmer knew what fate awaited them if they crossed paths with Goody and Betty Wee. They had a choice, really, a simple choice:

unveil the contents of their cart and let the Wee witches take their pick of all their wares. Or—if they refused—they would continue their journey with dread, knowing that the cart, when they least expected it, would overturn in a spectacular fashion, spilling all its contents. The entire load would be lost—and, if the Wee witches were in a particularly foul temper, the farmer's life would be lost as well.

It wasn't much of a choice at all, really.

Perhaps most chilling of all was how much the Wee witches delighted in their evildoings. Not even the roaring Nineveh Falls could drown out their gleeful cackles.

Why should the Wee witches work an honest day, when their malicious mischief was so much more fun?

CHAPTER 5

The Cursed Treasure of Charles Island

Charles Island has long been a site with an air of otherworldly menace about it, but what Captain William Kidd did there in 1699 is among the worst acts of evil the island has ever seen. Is it any wonder that his curse has lingered there for more than three hundred years?

Captain Kidd was a notorious pirate who terrorized the seas, looting and pillaging and striking fear into the hearts of even the bravest sailors. His criminal crew was just as fearsome—but they, too, harbored dread in their hearts of what Captain Kidd could do.

His crimes were so terrible, and his reputation so notorious, that authorities came up with a plan to capture Kidd once and for all in a desperate attempt to restore order to the high seas. They started an elaborate rumor that if only Kidd would journey to Boston, he would receive a full pardon for all his crimes.

The trap was set. And Captain Kidd found the bait irresistible.

Just because a pardon awaited him (or so he thought), Kidd had no intention of putting an end to his crimes. His ship was loaded down will ill-gotten cargo as he sailed up the Atlantic coast. He had two items on his agenda: To boast about his upcoming pardon and to bury his loot so that he could safely retrieve it later.

Charles Island was a deserted piece of land just half a mile off the coast of Milford, Connecticut. Of course, Captain Kidd wouldn't have cared if he needed to slaughter a few residents to accomplish his goal. But the seclusion of the island was part of its appeal.

The wooden chest was secured with iron fastenings, which would have made it heavy to carry even when it was empty. The chest, though, was far from empty. It was filled to the brim with shiny gold coins and glittering jewels in a rainbow of colors. Just a small handful of the loot would be enough for one of Captain Kidd's men to live in luxury for the rest of his days. But none of the pirates were foolish enough to dream of doing such a thing. After all, no one knew better than them what Captain Kidd could do. And he was especially vicious with thieves and traitors.

Captain Kidd marched across the sandy shore of Charles Island while his men followed, struggling to transport the weighty chest. No one knew precisely what Captain Kidd was looking for as he scanned the empty island.

But when he found it, he knew.

"Here," he might have said as he pointed to a secluded, wooded spot, not visible from the shore unless you knew exactly what you were looking for.

Then he stood back and watched as his crew began to dig.

One shovelful at a time, earth flew through the air as the hole grew deeper and deeper. Only Captain Kidd knew how deep he wanted it. For their part, the men didn't mind the labor of digging the hole, even when their shovels scraped against flinty stones or gnarled roots.

They were grateful for anything that might delay what would happen next.

But it was impossible the delay the inevitable. All too soon, it seemed, Captain Kidd was satisfied with the depth of the pit his men had dug. It was deep enough to hold the treasure chest.

And deep enough to hold something else, too.

Perhaps Captain Kidd said something like, "That's a fine depth."

Or perhaps he just nodded his head.

His crew was silent as they stood around the hole, their shovels still, their heads bowed.

Now, for the moment they had secretly dreaded: It was time for drawing lots.

One of them held out his fist, which clutched a handful of sticks. There was one for each member of the crew. From the look of it, each stick was the same length.

But the men already knew that was an illusion.

If they were afraid, they didn't show it. With bluster and bravado, each man reached for a stick.

Each man reached for his fate.

The sticks were the same length—all except for one. The man who chose the short stick knew what that meant.

Maybe he tried to smile. Maybe he tried to act brave. Maybe he said something like, "Let's get it over with, then."

Captain Kidd's sword was sharp and swift. It was a flash of silver as it sliced through the air.

As it sliced through the man's throat.

He fell to his knees almost before the blood bubbled out of the gash in his neck. Dead in an instant, his body tumbled into the hole, sprawled across the treasure chest. His blood soaked into the wood of the chest. It pooled in the bottom of the pit.

His skin was still warm when the first shovelfuls of earth rained down on him. Buried with the treasure, Captain Kidd was certain his slain sailor's spirit would guard it as ferociously as he would were he still alive.

By the time the dirty job was done, it was low tide, and the sandbar connecting Charles Island to the town of Milford had been revealed. Captain Kidd didn't spare another thought for the murdered mate as he marched across the sandbar with the rest of the men and paraded through the town. The pardon he had been promised was so close he could practically taste it.

But Captain Kidd himself was in for a nasty surprise.

When he arrived in Boston, he was swiftly arrested, tried, and convicted of piracy. Two years later, he met his own fate at the end of a hangman's noose. Captain Kidd died without ever revealing where his treasure was buried. Now Kidd's restless spirit also guarded his long-buried loot.

Whispered rumors persisted about the treasure that lingered under the soil of Charles Island. Even after a hundred years, the thought of discovering a bounty of stolen pirate loot was appealing enough that two men were willing to risk everything in their pursuit of Captain Kidd's long-lost treasure. In 1838, they stole onto Charles Island, moving swiftly and stealthily so that no one would see them.

Then they started to dig.

And dig.

And dig.

Eventually, their relentless quest for pirate treasure paid off in the sound of a loud, dull *thwack*: the noise of spade striking solid wood.

The men stared at each other in shock and disbelief.

They dug faster, more furiously, eventually tossing their shovels to the side and scraping handfuls of dirt off the aged chest. Forgetting all about stealth and secrecy, the men pitched the dirt over their shoulders. They were so fixated on the idea that they'd soon be richer than their wildest dreams that they didn't even notice the old, yellowed bones.

At last, the chest was cleared of dirt and debris. Sparks flew as they began to stab the padlock with their spades. All they had to do was break the rusty lock and the riches would belong to them.

Or so they thought.

Suddenly, an ear-shattering shriek pierced the sky. The men dropped their spades and covered their ears from the deafening sound, which was like nothing they had ever heard before. They looked at the heavens only to behold a terrifying sight: a headless demon made entirely of moldering bones was flying at them at dizzying speed. The men scrambled out of the hole just before the demon descended into it, exploding in a burst of blue flames and choking smoke.

They didn't wait for the smoke to clear. The two men ran as fast as they could to escape from the island and Captain Kidd's curse, their hearts thundering in their chests.

In the light of a new day, though, the demon seemed less terrifying—at least, compared to the thought of forever abandoning the riches that the men had left behind. So they mustered all their courage and set off for Charles Island once more.

When they arrived, there was no sign of the demon.

And no sign of the treasure.

The deep hole they'd dug had been filled in as if by supernatural forces. There was no sign that the dirt had ever been disturbed. They dug

again, always keeping a watchful eye on the skies, always keeping an ear listening for that same tell-tale *thwack* of spade on wood.

After hours toiling in the sun, the men had dug a pit twice their height—far deeper than the one they had dug just the day before. It was no use to continue. They left Charles Island with far more questions than they'd had when they first arrived.

Who had moved the treasure?

Who had filled in the hole?

Perhaps Captain Kidd knows the answer.

But dead men tell no tales.

The Bride and
the Soldier

A terrible sadness descended upon the Daniel Benton Homestead in 1777. It is a cloud of grief and longing so thick that it still lingers. Two young lovers who encountered great trials and tribulations in life, only to be cruelly separated by death, linger there, too.

Daniel Benton's grandson, Elisha, fell in love with pretty Jemima Barrows as soon as he saw her. Jemima was much younger than Elisha— more than ten years—but that did nothing to stop his powerful affection for her. Alas, from the first moment Elisha laid eyes on Jemima, their love was doomed, as they hailed from different social classes. The Benton family was well-to-do, while Jemima's father was only a cabinetmaker. The Bentons would never approve a union between Elisha and Jemima.

But love knows no such practicalities, and Elisha vowed that one day he would make Jemima his wife. When Jemima returned his affections and accepted his secret proposal, Elisha knew that his dreams would come true. Even as he enlisted in the army and prepared to fight in the Revolutionary War, Elisha's heart was light. Someday, he knew, the war would end. Someday he would return home.

Someday he would return to Jemima, and they would build a beautiful life together.

Unfortunately, Elisha was only partly right.

While Elisha was at war, Jemima stayed home

and dreamed of their future. She carefully filled her hope chest with linens and other necessities they would need in their new home. Perhaps she even sewed a bridal gown to wear on their wedding day. All these preparations, she believed, would help the time go faster until the war ended and Elisha returned to her.

During the Battle of Long Island, Elisha and two of his brothers were captured by British forces and forced onto a prison ship that was anchored near Brooklyn, New York.

The conditions on the ship were deplorable. Men were crammed into crowded spaces aboard the ship, with little fresh air and less room to move. There was not enough food to go around, and all too often the food was rotten or infested by rodents. The stench was unbearable.

It's no wonder that, when the dreaded smallpox virus arrived on the ship, it tore through the prisoners like a wildfire. One by one, Elisha's brothers became ill and succumbed to the deadly disease.

Then it was Elisha's turn.

His skin burned with fever. Blisters in his mouth and throat made it impossible for him to swallow, let alone eat or drink. Fluid-filled sores erupted all over his body, leaking pus onto his bedclothes.

When it came time for the British forces to select a prisoner for exchange, the ailing Elisha was an easy choice. After all, they figured, he'd be dead soon enough anyway.

The cart that carried Elisha back to the Benton House rattled over the roads. Elisha moaned softly, only half aware of what was happening and where he was going.

His family should have rejoiced to welcome Elisha home. But as soon as they saw how gravely ill he was, their celebrations turned into preparations of a different sort. Knowing all too well that smallpox was extremely contagious, they immediately walled off a section of the house where Elisha would quarantine all alone while everyone waited for him to survive the virus—or succumb.

Elisha wasn't alone for long. As soon as word reached Jemima that her beloved had returned, she made haste to the Benton home, where she discovered Elisha in a sorry state. The Bentons warned Jemima that she must not go near him or risk catching the contagion, but she refused to heed their pleas, pushing past them to enter the quarantine room without delay.

Elisha, through his feverish haze, recognized his betrothed and smiled weakly.

Jemima dropped to the floor and took his hot, dry hand in hers. She kissed it and reached for the washbasin, where she wrung out a rag and pressed it to Elisha's chapped lips.

It was the first drop of water he'd had in hours.

Soon after, Jemima's parents arrived to offer their prayers of support to the Benton family in their time of need. Oh, the horror Mr. and Mrs. Barrows felt when they realized their precious daughter had arrived at the Benton house before them—and had exposed herself to the terrible contagion! They refused to go near her or let her come home. There was little hope for Jemima now, they feared.

As for Jemima? She wasn't afraid. She wouldn't have gone home even if her parents had welcomed her with open arms. She knew where she belonged: at the bedside of her betrothed.

Elisha lingered for days, and true to her word, Jemima never faltered in her devotion— not even when the first flush of fever crept into her cheeks and the aches settled into her bones. When he died on January 21, Jemima was still with him, still holding his hand.

His family, still so terrified of the dreadful virus that had taken Elisha's life, had his lifeless body passed through a window in his tiny quarantine room rather than carry it through the rest of the house and spread contagion from room to room.

They did not take down the makeshift wall they'd built—not yet.

For now Jemima lay atop Elisha's deathbed, burning with fever, covered from head to toe with weeping, crusted pox.

She lingered for more than a month, suffering just as Elisha did. Perhaps Jemima suffered even worse, because through the throes of her illness there was no one there to wipe her brow or hold her hand.

Jemima Barrows died all alone.

Since Jemima and Elisha had never had the opportunity to get married, they could not be buried beside each other. A road separates them in death, just as war, strife, and sickness separated them in life.

Perhaps this cruel burial arrangement was the final indignity that Jemima and Elisha would be forced to suffer.

Perhaps this is why they cannot rest peacefully in their graves.

Not long after Elisha and Jemima passed from this world to the next, members of the Benton family began to hear ghostly footsteps echoing through the corridors, even when no one was moving. Sometimes the hearth began to glow as if a warm blaze crackled within it—even when there was no fire.

Sometimes, the figure of a woman in a bridal gown is seen, gliding from one room to the next.

Sometimes, the specter of a Colonial soldier is spotted pacing the halls, almost as if he is searching for someone.

Even visitors to the distanced graves of Elisha and Jemima can feel a deep sense of sadness settle over them—or a creeping sense of unease as though someone were watching them from beyond.

Perhaps it is the spirits of Jemima and Elisha themselves, wondering if someone, anyone, will acknowledge their love at last.

Tory Den

Not all the colonists believed in the cause of the Revolutionary War. British loyalists were called Tories, and they believed that England was far too powerful to rise against. As a result of their loyalty to the British Crown, the Tories were hated by the Revolutionaries.

There was such a large number of Tories in Connecticut that the Revolutionaries feared they endangered the future of the United States. The Revolutionaries had to hunt down the Tories to prevent them from sabotaging their battles for independence. Captured Tories were interrogated, punished, and subjected to conversion tactics that were so fearful they were spoken of only in whispers. Even if a Tory was cleared of treason, he faced abuse and harassment from his neighbors. There were reports of Tories being shot at or tarred and feathered. A Tory convicted of treason faced the prospect of death by hanging.

Is it any wonder the Tories did everything they could to avoid capture?

The Tory Dens, located throughout Connecticut, were perhaps their most important secret weapon.

This network of caves provided a safe shelter for Tories when revolutionaries searched for them from door to door and town to town. Tory wives kept a careful eye on the roads, watching for any sign that a band of revolutionaries, such as the Sons of Liberty, was on the march. If she spotted them, she might stand on the doorstep and blow into a conch shell. The low, mournful tone carried an urgent message: Hide!

Any Tories in the area who heard the cry of the conch shell knew what they had to do. Leaving their tools in the fields and their horses still saddled, the Tories would rush to the nearest Tory Den. With swift, silent steps they would approach the closest cave and slip through its gaping mouth into the secret shelter of the darkness within.

Then they would wait.

One of the most famous—or perhaps infamous—Tory Dens was a unique structure created when a massive slab of rock fell onto two other large stones, creating a natural chamber that appeared to have no entrance—unless you knew where to look. This Tory Den had a southeast entrance and an even more secretive central entrance that was just large enough for a person to squeeze through. At the north end, there was a cramped and tiny opening that was almost too small to use as an entrance.

Almost.

How many Tories would cram together in this hard, lonesome space? How long would they wait for a sign that the Sons of Liberty had moved on to other targets in other areas? Were they afraid? Were they hungry? Were they cold? Did they look at that small opening in the center of the cave and imagine building a small fire beneath, where they could warm their stiff, numb fingers?

Of course, they wouldn't dare build a fire. The puffs of smoke that spiraled out would be a sure giveaway.

The hours must have felt endless. No one spoke a word for fear of being heard; the stony chamber had strange acoustics that could make even a whisper echo like a shout. Perhaps, if it wasn't too dangerous, one of the wives would sneak away to the cave with a basket of food and water. How grateful the hiding men must have been to see her. To have something to eat. To have a sign that there was still a world outside this miserable cave, a world with family and food and sunlight. A world to which they might soon return and live freely and openly—if they were lucky.

One of the hardest parts of being a Tory sympathizer in New England must have been the relentlessness of the winters. Imagine the freezing caves during a harsh winter storm. Even a stack of carefully stashed woolen blankets and furs would do little to ward off the icy winds and bitter chill that seemed to seep into the rocky sides of the cave. It must've been hard, in the bleakest, darkest days of winter, for the Tories not to imagine that the cave was all too similar to a tomb. Dark, and still, and cold. So very, very cold.

There is record of just one Tory being hanged for treason, but the fear that all Tories lived under during the years of the Revolutionary War likely changed them forever. Their senses were always alert. At any moment, they were watching the road for danger; listening for the warning of the conch shell; crouching in the damp recesses of the cave, willing their hearts not to beat quite so loud or so fast. The interminable hours in the cave . . . waiting . . . waiting . . . waiting for capture or waiting for the moment to leave and risk everything. To return home, which meant returning to life on highest alert.

The Tories are long dead, but the tensions and emotions they carried with them into the caves live on. Many hikers and explorers have reported seeing misty figures at the cave entrances, slinking in and out. There are, at times, odd lights for which no human explanation can be found. Could they be ghostly fires that the shivering Tories once longed to start?

Voices still echo off the stone walls, and even the sounds of heavy, panicked breathing can be heard by those who listen carefully. Most tellingly, visitors to the Tory Dens report a heavy, fearful presence that seems to infect them like a pathogen until they can bear it no longer and escape from the caves as quickly as possible.

Perhaps even the stone walls of the caves absorbed the heightened emotions of the Tories who sought shelter and sanctuary within. Like the damp condensation that brings such chill to the caves, all that fear and anxiety beads upon the stone walls and ceilings, dripping invisible droplets of terror onto all who gather in the Tory Dens.

Drip.

Drip.

Drip.

Fort Griswold's Gruesome Ghosts

Sometimes places become haunted by spirits who cannot move on from their earthly lives to the realm beyond. Sometimes places become haunted because a terrible crime happened there.

Sometimes, it's both.

The Revolutionary War was a time of great bravery and triumph. A new country was born upon the ideals of independence. But like all wars, the Revolutionary War showcased some of the worst elements of human behavior. Cowardice, betrayal, treason, treachery.

And even massacres.

Fort Griswold was constructed to provide protection to the harbor, ships, and towns of Groton and New London. On September 6, 1781, the British invaded Groton and New London, burning the towns one building at a time until the sky was black with smoke and the flames cast such terrible heat that no one could set foot in either town.

The devastation, though, was just beginning.

As the towns burned, British lieutenant colonel Edmund Eyre led eight hundred troops to Fort Griswold. With the blazes raging and the smoke billowing through the sky, it was clear that the British forces had triumphed. When Colonel Eyre reached Fort Griswold, he acted according to all codes of military honor by sending forth a flag to demand a peaceful surrender.

Twice, the Revolutionaries refused.

Their commander, Colonel William Ledyard, was certain that reinforcements were on the

way. He was determined to hold the fort until they arrived—even if it cost the life of every last man under his command.

His grave miscalculations would haunt Fort Griswold for centuries to come.

At last, Colonel Eyre ran out of patience. He issued one more warning.

When no surrender was forthcoming, the British stormed Fort Griswold.

The two sides were not evenly matched. The British forces numbered 800, while only 150 Revolutionaries were holed up within the walls of the fort.

But the first wave of the attack proved lethal for the British, as many soldiers were killed in their attempts to cross the deep ditch in front of the fort. Eventually, however, the British forces persevered and were able to invade. They forced open the heavy gates and marched right in.

Despite being outnumbered more than four to one, Colonel Ledyard and his men made a brave show of attempting to hold off the British soldiers. Within forty minutes, though, the battle was over. Colonel Ledyard had no choice but to surrender.

Perhaps Colonel Ledyard had already forgotten his own refusal to play by the rules of war when Colonel Eyre and his men first approached Fort Griswold.

Or perhaps Colonel Ledyard thought that the rules should apply to everyone but him.

Regardless, it must have been a terribly unpleasant surprise when he presented his sword to Colonel Eyre in the customary gesture of honorable surrender—only to have Colonel Eyre turn Ledyard's own sword on him, killing him immediately!

The rest of the British forces showed no mercy to the remaining Revolutionary troops, killing most of them where they stood.

Then the British troops dumped the wounded soldiers into an artillery cart so that they could quickly—if not carefully—transport them out of Fort Griswold. Why the rush? Well, the British wanted to blow up the fort's ammunition before Revolutionary reinforcements could arrive and reclaim it.

The cart, piled high with the wounded and the dying, must have been a miserable ride as it bumped and bounced along the road. Then the unthinkable happened. The British forces lost control of the cart, which careened down the hillside before crashing into a cluster of trees. The moans and screams of the wounded could be heard clear across the river.

Of course, Americans remember the incident slightly differently. They claim the British did it on purpose.

The crash was so severe that several of the wounded died in the wreck. The rest were hauled over to British prisoner ships and held captive in the same terrible conditions that led to the death of Elisha Benton.

It is astonishing that any of them survived.

Though the exact numbers are unknown, it is widely believed that eighty-five American soldiers and fifty-one British troops died on that fateful day at Fort Griswold. Their bodies were dumped in a shallow mass grave at the gates of the fort, barely covered by a thin layer of dirt.

Is it any wonder their spirits have been restless all these years?

Fort Griswold is now a museum, where the sword of Colonel Ledyard—wiped clean of his blood—is on display. That's not all that's on display at Fort Griswold. Many people have reported hearing the voices of soldiers long dead. Strange orbs sometimes appear within the fort, glowing ominously. Often, a foreboding mist rises from the ground.

The battle for Fort Griswold ended centuries ago. But for the soldiers who fought and died there, it's still going on.

Afterword

These chilling tales, each haunting in its own unique way, are bonded by a common location: the Great State of Connecticut, which is home to more specters, haunts, and legends than the pages of this book could contain. These mysteries, and many more, await all who set foot in Connecticut. Perhaps you will someday encounter the Green Lady or the Headless Horseman or even the Black Dog of the Hanging Hills. Each one carries a message from beyond—a message that is as essential as it is mysterious.

Maybe that's something else that bonds these spooky stories together: an underlying longing to communicate. To connect. After all,

it's possible that each one of these mysteries could be solved—and each one of these spirits finally laid to an eternal and peaceful rest—if the right person was listening.

Perhaps that person could be you.